I0825094

HOW BEAUTIFUL PEOPLE ARE

a pothi by Ayaz Pirani

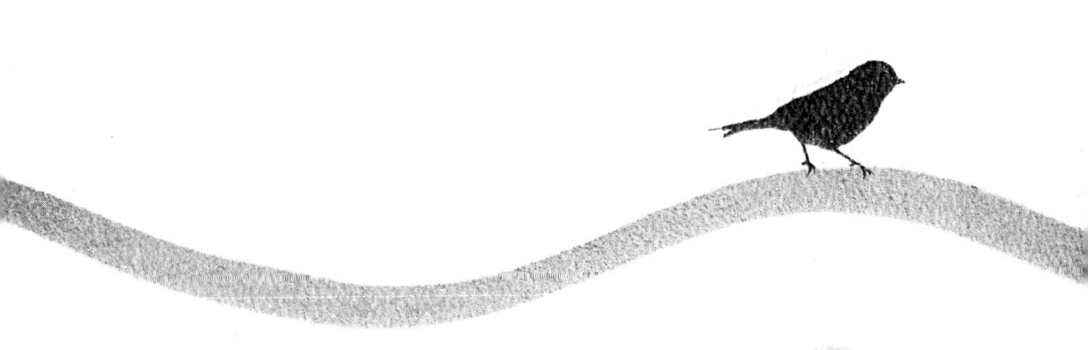

Edited by Shane Neilson
Cover and book design by Jeremy Luke Hill
Proofreading by Carol Dilworth
Set in Linux Libertine
Printed on Mohawk Via Felt
Printed and bound by Arkay Design & Print

LIBRARY AND ARCHIVES CANADA CATALOGUING IN PUBLICATION

Title: How beautiful people are / a pothi by Ayaz Pirani.
Names: Pirani, Ayaz, author.
Description: Poems.
Identifiers: Canadiana (print) 20210370483 | Canadiana (ebook) 20210370505 |
ISBN 9781774220504 (softcover) | ISBN 9781774220573 (HTML) |
ISBN 9781774220511 (PDF)
Classification: LCC PS8631.I71 H69 2022 | DDC C811/.6—dc23

Gordon Hill Press gratefully acknowledges the support of the Ontario Arts Council.

Gordon Hill Press respectfully acknowledges the ancestral homelands of the Attawandaron, Anishinaabe, Haudenosaunee, and Métis Peoples, and recognizes that we are situated on Treaty 3 territory, the traditional territory of Mississaugas of the Credit First Nation.

Gordon Hill Press also recognizes and supports the diverse persons who make up its community, regardless of race, age, culture, ability, ethnicity, nationality, gender identity and expression, sexual orientation, marital status, religious affiliation, and socioeconomic status.

Gordon Hill Press
130 Dublin Street North
Guelph, Ontario, Canada
N1H 4N4
www.gordonhillpress.com

for Mom and Dad, Ami and Abbu

etali re sudh budh chande suraj didhi

TABLE OF CONTENTS

BELOVED INFIDEL

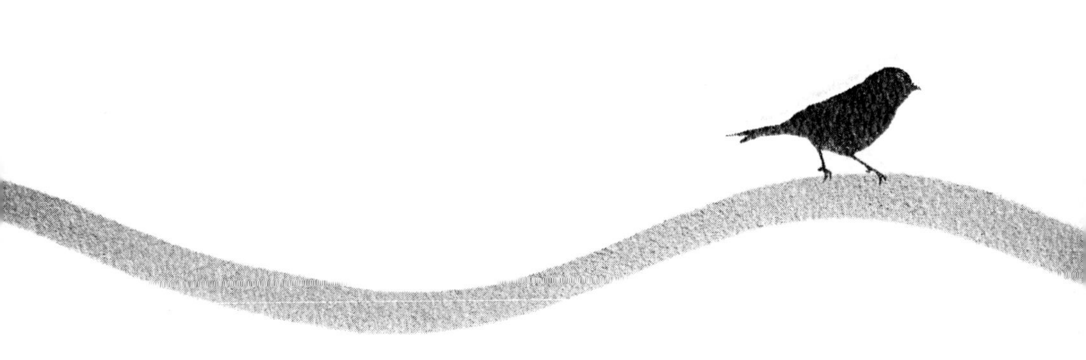

Written With the Other Hand

No space for grief.
Potted plant people

talk their quota
and friends wave

without using their arms.
I make my dictionary face.

If something is said
I snap like a flag

then flag like
an adjournment.

I'm in the room
but as the broom.

Historical Disadvantage

Long

have I lived among
white people.

Tell me I'm the lucky one
while I weep

at the Xerox
or curl up

with the other grains of sand.
I'd like to think

I'm living on the edge.
On a dog-eared page.

Nutshells

Like the leaf curl,
as the bee wing.

Better an alibi of birds
than congregating with stars.

Fall for the held breath
in warm stone

or a plainspoken door.
Love may not be straight

or forward
like a shirt buttons.

As decided as water
come to boil.

Ali's Tiger

I.

My language is abridged, thin
like a Bible's paper.

I'm trying to print
but not be two-sided.

Kiss me the way a plane skids.
It'll be like horses in the garden.

Imagine one broom holding
another broom.

Or the historical disadvantage
of two grains of sand.

II.

How many leaves in the forest?
How many men's suits in the city?

There's no end to the tangles
in a guru's beard.

Ali's tiger won't let you count its stripes.
Might as well interrogate the wave.

While most words curl like leaves
I know a few the ear doesn't hear.

Are you done shaking hands with thin ice,
kissing snowdrift to snowdrift?

III.

Imagine a drawer of ornithology.
Long arms, some words.

Beloved Infidel

Who wants to be blown to pieces
or get placed under wraps?

Don't get bottled like a scent.
Walk into the forest newly born.

In your face there's sunken treasure.
A band of sleeping merry men.

If you go out with a bang
you won't end up in a thousand gardens.

Nakalanki

I went to the house where you were born
and it was filled with birdsong.

The rains came down and purified nothing.
Some birds cried like cats prowl.

Now when we ask for memory
we end up with a pile of men's suits.

I thought you said 3rd floor, Muhammad Ali, Karachi
but it looks more like Nakalanki's navel.

The face of a rock-dashed hope.
The swagger of interrogated nostalgia.

You made it out of the burning building.
From its touches you were born.

Entropomorphist

I.

The pillows on the bed
accept the day's arrangement.

The chairs pose.
In the closet the broom

has its own broom.
The lamp isn't cornered.

II.

Afreen's in the garden
but it's an inquest.

Snail's on the run
for what it's done.

Newt knows
while worm splits.

Stone sets
aside its feelings.

Childless

I.

Too late
is on time.

II.

From a hundred
good reasons

to a few chewed
feelings.

III.

We’re side by side
but like shelved books.

Sita & Ram

I never wanted to go mirror to mirror.
Now I'll have to be a wisp of smoke.
I hope the point doesn't dull.
It's not enough that I lived with a demon
and embraced only the fleeting image.
Right now I'd rather be a fleeting image.
This year's bird is not in last year's nest.
Who wants to make burning coals speak?
Not only impurities are burnt in fire.
Buds and blossoms too are blackened.

In a Good Way

I.

You forget the couplet
has two arms.

What you need to know
comes from observing the moon.

Better now that the silence
is scented.

II.

Trees
have friendship.

Loving lichens,
listless browns.

Your hair
is a necropolis.

I Spend My Life Learning About Myself What She Sees in a Glance

I point the way a dog points.

Charro del Valle

The year Pedro went ranching in Oaxaca
I pressed the starched bluejeans at the laundry.

The rivets made hot commemorations
and the buttons polished off my fingertips.

I ended up with a signature caress.
Touch of wide sky, nose-rub of sage.

Sat Panth

Faced with a thousand
dogs off-leash

I live among
white people.

I teach their young chairs
and blowdryers.

They also know me
by vignette.

An undiscovered country.
Described abridged.

Things I lost
had to go.

DEATH TO AMERICA

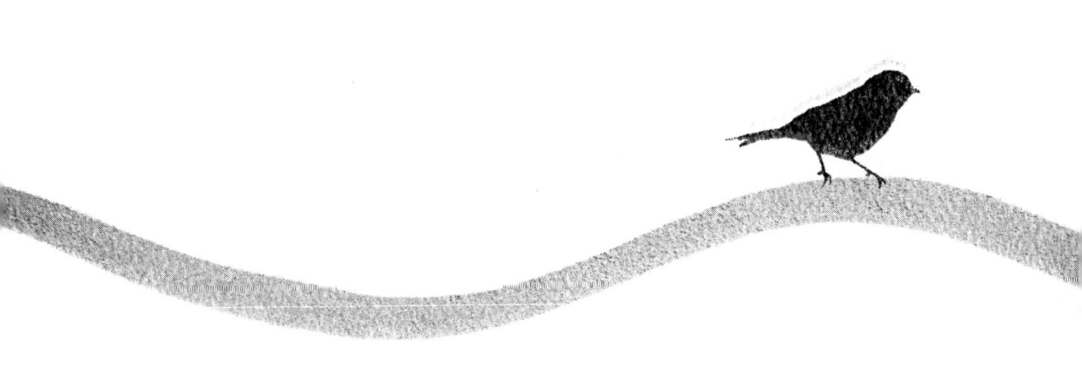

The Door's Not Talking

When has the bookshelf
been so quiet?

It's the sofa's choice
whether to abstain.

Even from its interrogation posture
the chair won't budge.

The lamp is cornered.
Who will light the room?

Back to the wallpaper
and on the rug's schedule

the mirror's got nothing
to offer.

Saith the Missionary

Long

ago my lentils boiled.
I'm so glad to be an artifact

and not a ruin.
The past is laminated.

I'm here to learn how
beautiful people are.

Teach me gem's charm
but also rose's wilt.

I'm on the path of
the one on a path.

Poem for My Grandmother

She built a home from dung.
She buried cat placenta.
She won't lie down
wherever you put her.
She's unlikely to bend
from tradition's pinch.
After so many years off Eglinton
she'll brook no guff.
Won't comfort crooked.
Her best lines are one syllable.

In Kitchener Jamatkhana, 1976

I got to know the carpet
by individual thread.

Some went against the grain,
most were seaward.

I was shy in my socks,
black and formal

that put me in my dad's shoes.
Pant cuffs, I learned, show

what you've been through.
Some kids had it easy

and sat single-mindedly.
Others were chopped trees.

I liked it when my hands
displayed human joy or dog's sleep.

At the tasbih's fumko
a promise was knot.

Ontario

I put the lake on notice
and said goodbye.

It wasn't just a blue face
speaking plain speech.

The lake was full stop.
Wide and deep.

My father had Victoria
to lean on

something massive like
childhood grief

that lets you charm
other earthlings.

I licked a two-scoop,
watched parasols parade.

I put the lake on notice
and said goodbye.

Sat Gur

I'm led by an unattached hand.
Not the kind that turns the page

or draws up the blanket.
It's not that attached to me.

It won't lend me its hand.
It's more of a hand that points

with fingers that snap.
Never known it to reach out.

Umed & Sheru

With whom should I become friends
if all the world shall pass away?
— Sri Guru Granth Sahib

I.

One was called
but two came along.

Now she's a floating image.
He's a wisp of smoke.

When their portion came
they broke the fast.

True Guru led them into the forest.
His ginans please the birds.

II.

Running into burning buildings
they showed owl's indifference.

The thread is four continents long
and ends at the gate of yearning.

The thrift of our own lives
puts their narrative to shame.

III.

Both were hard-headed.
Eaters of wisdom-pearls.

What was once a whole
became part of another whole.

Grain of sand
rubbed by grain of sand.

IV.

Each stiffened by the other's fire.
True path is to the ancestor's cave.

One was called
but two came along.

Ngorongoro

My grandfather was a man of other people's words. He had the face of a dictionary. Born in Gujarat, he died after four continents and five languages. He's been dead so long he's come alive in my dreams. When you're alone with your thoughts, you wish you had better thoughts. You wish you had somebody else's thoughts. I'm glad to be on Earth but it hasn't been a pleasure being myself. Too far from the source, a man who walked forward like his back was against the wall. Now that he's gone I've fallen into the crater. There's no good fortune in historical disadvantage. It's so hard for one grain of sand to fall in love with another grain of sand.

Kilimanjaro

My grandmother was a child of Empire. All the rooms she entered were divided, where could the foot be planted? No one falls in love with the cornered lamp. She had the face of a rock hopes dash on. You expected her to make it out of any burning building. All the pages of my people's pothi are in her memory. The whole story takes place between my mother tongue and my grandmother's tongue. Even if all I have left is the faintest idea.

Origins

From a touch
you were born.

Not on bee wing
or at leaf's curl

or by a word the ear
doesn't hear.

From a touch
you were born.

Grain of sand rubbed
grain of sand.

Broom danced
with broom.

From a touch
you were born.

Where Are You From?

There's no road to my village.
The language they speak
is to not speak to me.
I might catch a glimpse
but it'll be a figment.
Where both the moon and the sun
hang in the sky, rain falls

but doesn't know where to fall.
All my ancestors are stone-faced.
I'm like a child who's born
and then dies on the same day.
It won't be the first time
I'm not going home again.
A pleasure to meet you.

Royal Ontario Museum

After opening or closing
drawers of ornithology or anthropology

I worried my own past might get laminated or eliminated.
Who wants to be numbered or alphabetized?

Subject to or of
a thousand autopsies or empires?

Imagine ending up a bottled scent or a dog's breath.
Some rose or some cardamom.

Some or all
post-colonial loss or personal list.

POC RSVP

At the party I'd like to be a person of interest
but will end up a person of colour.
Instead of agency I'll get stuck with adjacency.
I worship in gutters, dust ignores me.
Imagine the roar of a lion's mouth
or a perch on the rim of Ngorongoro.
I'm not coming to greet your waves.
I won't dance broom to broom.
Don't ask me to breathe fire or starve a child.
I'm not shaking hands with wilted roses
or standing two-headed like scissors.
I'd rather retreat at the first balloon's pop.

OEDAF

I've got a thousand
cuts from pages

of the Queen's English.
Always a dictionary

walking by
who'll reach out

to straighten
my nose.

Death to America

My voice doesn't curdle blood.
My fist doesn't rattle the air.

I don't even know the words
to *Death to America.*

Why does it bother you
if I whip my own back?

You think the mood might strike
to deliver the worst gift?

The crater I'll leave behind
is an unwrapped rose,

uninterrupted
like Ngorongoro.

POC QED

Chalk on the black.
Scar is the story.

I’m but a briefcase.
Kept best in pocket.

On the longish list for
one of a kind.

Either end of the pencil.
I’m done being me,

problem solved.
No point

passing by
just to hang out

(poof or proof
I don’t know)

in the margin
as a theorem.

(WHITE) CITY | KID (TROPIC)

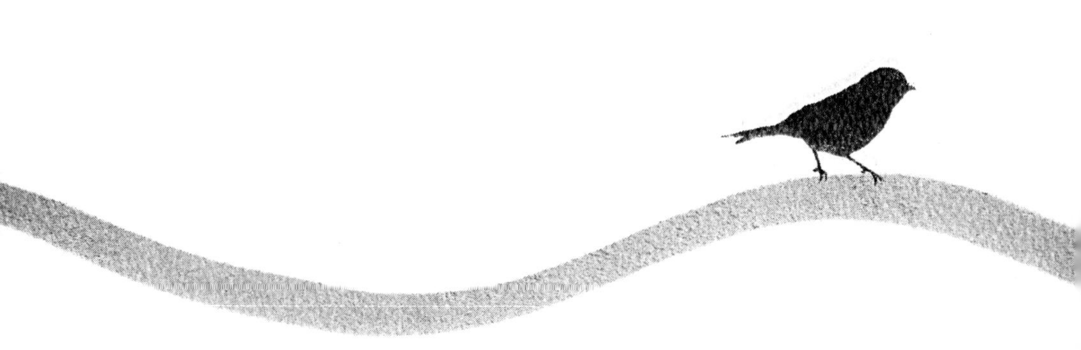

I.

An army of blowdryers
has left the city

unbuttoned.
The mayor called

for a congregation
of birds

and got a pile of
men's suits.

II.

Figures are bleak.
Rich people

are losing money.
Poor people are losing

people.
Once in skyscrapers

the steak-eaters
now eat street urchins.

III.

I'm alone
with mango pickle

and Lata's *Lata.*
I'm done

shaking hands with
thin ice,

kissing snowdrift
to snowdrift.

IV.

I’ve lost track of the garden, no one breaks up with doubt.

V.

My ancestors aren't talking.
There's just piles of piles. Men's suits, a car forest.
Good morning, snowdrift. How's thin ice?

My friendships are room-specific.
I teach my young chairs and my office plants
listen to their foghorns.

People are shaped by glass rectangles
and halved by ajar doors.
Winter flakes off in the hallway.
Easy to ignore the cornered lamp.

VI.

In and out of buildings.
In and out of books.
In and out of countries.
When will this broom get its own broom?
When is maximum?

VII.

Let down by the automatically locked door
I thump the obscuring glass.
My jacket doesn't need my grief buttoning, unbuttoning.
I'm crushed by the white outside
and Rue Guy's downhill.

Not stitched to this place or any place.
There's no road to my village.

KABIR'S LONELINESS

You can't mistake a broom for part of the furnishing of a room as long as you use it to clean the furniture.

— Ludwig Wittgenstein

Other Muslim Bans

No selling snails door to door.
No depictions of the closet.
An end to crooked dance floors.
Full stop on larded bullets.
No map or merry making.
Don't swallow the golden key.
Your fidgeting is on notice.
No single grain of sand.
It's over for mild punishments.
You've had your last laugh.
No roseless gardens.
No firmer handshakes.
That countdown was final.
Probably end of page.
Cruel world says goodbye.
Nuance is heading for the door.

Pub Speech, Bamburi Hotel, 1958

I'm on the last leg of
someone else's journey.
The first stage began
before the birth of everyone
I've ever known.
Once you leave the village
there's no road back.
You can't cut corners or roll dice
with your ancestors.
Their gods are real
but don't speak.
Curtain rarely moves,
mirror's got nothing to offer;
what will darkness do
when True Guru makes light?

How Beautiful People Are

It's a wonder
how beautiful people are.

They are in themselves
like the shade or the sun

or the moonlight that
makes a regular person briefly

know how beautiful people are.
Though you wonder just

how beautiful people are?
What do they crave

and who fulfills them?
What if they're crying

and we've all been ignoring
how beautiful people are?

Childless

I.

Glad it was you stealing from the garden.
Glad those were your long, black, historical hairs.

II.

We could have had a few magic tricks of our own
but we ended up with nothing in our hands.

III.

We went too far down the path
before looking back.

Post-Colonial Loser

I'd like a serving of children's joy
with a night of dog's sleep.

I'd like to unwrap this body
and see the shivering histories

of the people who made my people.
It hasn't been a pleasure being me.

No flag for the undiscovered country.
I've hardly wrinkled the royal Nostril.

There'll be no mountain calm.
I'm on the milkmaid's schedule.

Language Arts

Face of a dog off-leash
I teach my potted plants.

Print but don't be two-sided.
Interrogate the wave.

Where can the foot be planted?
How beautiful people are.

I've nightingale's temperament
but salamander's task.

Kabir's Loneliness

I.

Where lions are arboreal
the birds don't fly.

Everyone leaves here full.
No one comes from there.

II.

A sea has grown in my house.
Where can the foot be planted?

No one breaks up with doubt.
I'm led by an unattached hand.

III.

The door's not talking.
There's no road to my village.

The couplet has two arms.
One is to fascinate the birds.

IV.

I'm not going to lie down
wherever I am put.

When will I empty my pockets
into the Ngorongoro Crater?

V.

My head is in the lion's mouth.
How long do I wait by this page?

No flag for the undiscovered country.
It's better to be lost than found.

VI.

Cut the root with the word.
I've lost track of my garden.

Sky is ripped above the house.
Crows do the laundry.

VII.

My face is mountain's calm
though I'm dangled from rope.

I've lost each friend I've made.
Behind me the whole world is stuck.

VIII.

One by one they join the pile of trees.
Instead of birds you get men's suits.

Against an army of blowdryers
each broom will need its own broom.

IX.

From a touch I was born.
I walk truth to truth.

Doubt talks to doubt.
Kabir watches Kabir.

POC RIP

List, lost.
Sindh, sand.

Notes

The opening epigraph is from the ginan *bindhraa re van maa sukh* by Pir Sadardin. Speaking roughly: most knowledge is taught by the sun and the moon. A treasury of ginans with audio recitals is available online from the University of Saskatchewan Library.

The last two lines of "Sita & Ram" are found in the short story "My Mother, Her Crime" by Ambai, translated by Lakshmi Holmström. The story is available in *Her Story So Far: Tales of the Girl Child in India,* edited by Monica Das.

The title of the poem "I Spend My Life Learning About Myself What She Sees in a Glance" is drawn from Philip Lopate, who was paraphrasing Carl Jung.

The verse from Sri Guru Granth Sahib is available at srigranth.org. English translation on this website is by Sardar Dr. Sant Singh Khalsa.

The quote from Ludwig Wittgenstein is found in *The Big Typescript.* I first learned of Wittgenstein's broom references in Ray Monk's biography *The Duty of Genius.*

The final couplet in "Language Arts" is from Ghalib.

Acknowledgements

"Sat Panth" is in issue 210 of *The Malahat Review.*

"Post-Colonial Loser" is in *Guest 16.*

"In Kitchener Jamatkhana, 1976" is in *Poetry Pause* from The League of Canadian Poets.

"POC RSVP" is in *AHVAZ//AAVAZ//AVAAZ,* a chapbook from The League of Canadian Poets.

"Ontario" is part of the "Tuesday poem" series on the dusie blog.

Bachelor of Art, a chapbook published by Anstruther Press, precedes this collection.

I'm grateful to Iain Higgins at *Malahat* for our brief exchange about paths and for wanting my poem. So many thanks to Kirby, poet, curator at Knife Fork Book, and editor of *Guest 16.* Thanks to editor Shazia Hafiz Ramji and bookmaker Nic Brewer for including me in the LCP Chapbook Series. I'm obliged to rob mclennan, conductor of the dusie blog. Thank you, Jim Johnstone and Anstruther Press, you gave me the goodwill to write the rest. Thank you to Shane and Jeremy at Gordon Hill Press. Good people making good books.

Mom and Dad, Ami and Abbu, all our family, our nephews and nieces, this book is for you, from Ayaz and Afreen. Also, for my two decades of students, my beloved infidels, I miss you all.

About the Author

Ayaz Pirani was born in Tanzania and studied Humanities in Toronto and Montreal. His degree is from Vermont College of Fine Arts. His books include *Happy You Are Here, Kabir's Jacket Has a Thousand Pockets*, and *Bachelor of Art.* His work has recently appeared in A*RC Poetry Magazine, The Antigonish Review, The Malahat Review*, and *Guest 16*. He lives near Monterey Bay, California.